I Wonder Wh...

Trees Have Leaves

and Other Questions About Plants

Andrew Charman

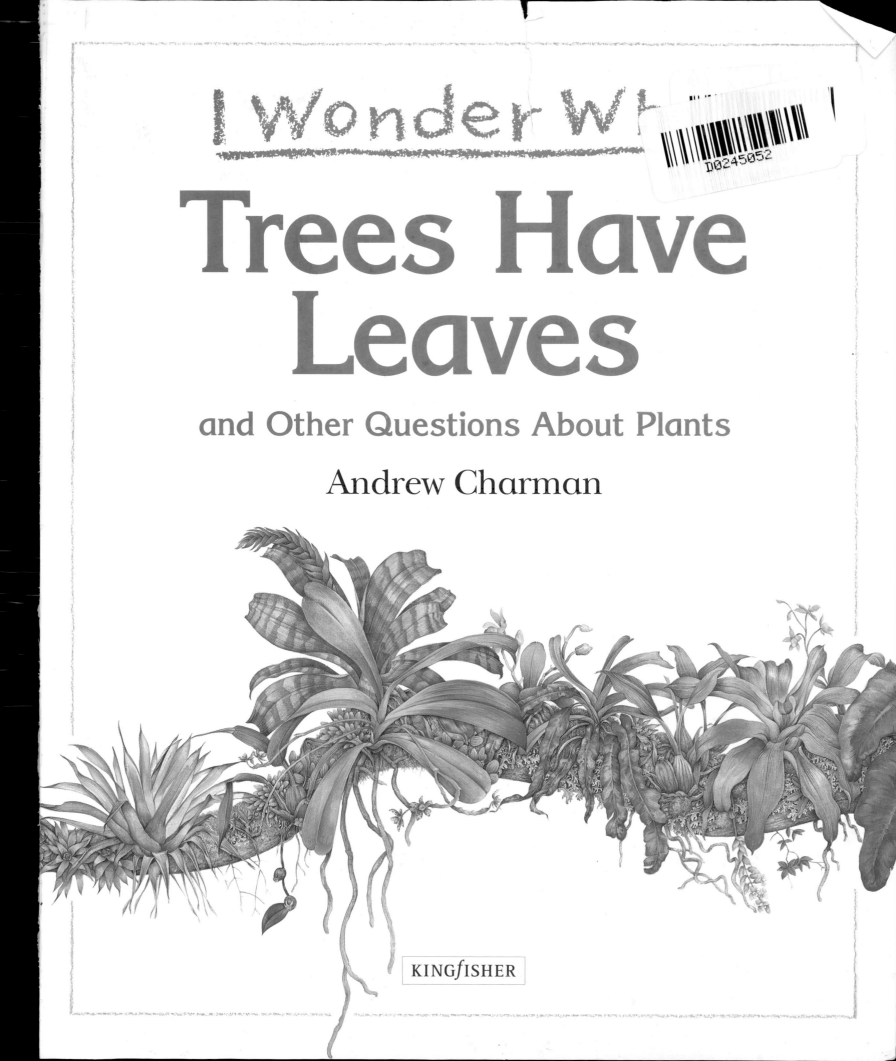

KING*fisher*

KINGFISHER
Kingfisher Publications Plc
New Penderel House
283–288 High Holborn
London WC1V 7HZ

First published by Kingfisher Publications Plc 1997
(hb) 10 9 8 7 6 5 4 3
(pb) 10 9 8 7 6 5 4
4TR(1GR)/0402/TIM/MAR/113 MA
Copyright © Kingfisher Publications Plc 1997

A CIP catalogue record for this book is
available from the British Library

ISBN 0 7534 0163 0 (hb)
        0 7534 0190 8 (pb)

Phototypeset by Tradespools Ltd, Frome, Somerset

Printed in China

Series editor: Clare Oliver
Series designer: David West Children's Books
Author: Andrew Charman
Consultant: Michael Chinery
Editor: Claire Llewellyn
Art editor: Christina Fraser
Picture researcher: Amanda Francis
Illustrations: Andrew Beckett (Garden Studio) 6–7; Peter
    Dennis (Linda Rogers) 28–29; Richard Draper 14–15;
    Chris Forsey cover, 8bm, 12–13, 30–31; Biz Hull (Artist
    Partners) 8–9; Ian Jackson 4–5, 16–17, 20–21, 26–27;
    Tony Kenyon (BL Kearley) all cartoons; Nicki Palin 10–11,
    24–25; Dan Wright 18–19, 22–23.

CONTENTS

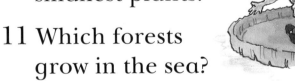

What is a plant?

Plants are living things. They come in all shapes and sizes, from tiny waterweeds to towering trees. Plants are different from animals in one very important way – they can make food for themselves from sunlight. Animals can't do this. They depend on plants for their food.

Where do plants grow?

There are about 380,000 different kinds of plants on Earth, and they grow just about everywhere – in fields and forests, deserts and mountains. Apart from air, the two things plants need are sunlight and water, so you won't find them in places that are completely dark or dry.

● All the food in the world starts with plants. You may eat eggs, meat and cheese but, without plants, no chicken or cow could produce these foods!

Are plants really alive?

Plants are just as alive as you are. They need air, food and water to grow, and they can make lots of new plants like themselves. This proves that they're alive. Things like stones and rocks don't feed, grow or have young because they're not alive.

● Corals and sea-anemones may look like plants, but they are imposters. In fact, they're animals!

Why do trees have leaves?

Like all plants, trees need their leaves to stay alive. Leaves are a tree's food factories. They contain a sticky green stuff called chlorophyll. The chlorophyll uses water, sunlight and carbon dioxide in the air to make a sugary food. The food is then carried to every part of the tree in a sweet and sticky juice called sap.

● If you've ever chewed a blade of grass, you'll know how sweet sap tastes. Hungry young caterpillars think so, too. That's why they eat leaves!

Why do some trees lose their leaves in autumn?

Big green leaves are useful in spring and summer. They make food while the sun shines and the days are long. When the days get shorter, there's less time for making food and the tree must live off its food reserves. Rather than feed their leaves too, some trees shed their leaves in autumn.

● The way plants make food in their leaves is called photosynthesis. During photosynthesis, plants take in carbon dioxide from the air. And they give out oxygen – the gas we all need to survive.

Why do leaves change colour in autumn?

● We call plants that lose their leaves in the autumn deciduous. Evergreens have tough leaves that can survive the winter. The trees still lose their leaves, but not all at the same time.

It's the chlorophyll in a plant's leaves that makes them look green. But in autumn, the chlorophyll breaks down. Once the green colouring has gone, the leaves' other colours show through – beautiful shades of red, yellow and gold.

Why do roots grow so long?

Long roots fix a plant firmly in the ground so that it won't fall over on windy days. But roots do another job, too. By spreading out far and wide, they can suck up water and goodness from all the soil around. Then the roots send the water up the stem or trunk and into the leaves.

● In the strongest winds, a tree can sometimes be blown right over. Its roots are wrenched out of the ground as the tree falls down with a crash.

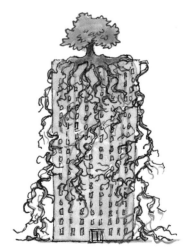

● A wild fig tree in South Africa grew roots 120 metres down into the soil. If it was put on the roof of a 40-storey office block, its roots would reach down to the ground.

● At the ends of the roots are tiny hairs, which burrow into the spaces between the lumps of soil.

● Sunflowers not only grow up towards the light, but their flowers follow the Sun! As the Sun appears to move across the sky through the day, the flower-heads turn to face it.

Why are stems so straight?

A plant needs to hold its leaves up to the sunshine, which it uses to make its food. Many plants grow tall, straight stems, so that they can beat their neighbours to the sunlight.

● Not all plants have straight stems. Some have stems that bend and curl, clambering their way over nearby plants as they climb up to the light.

Which plants grow in water?

The giant water lily grows in the lakes and rivers of South America. Its roots lie deep in the mud and its huge leaves float on the water's surface. This is the best place for catching the sun! Each leaf curls up at the rim so that it can push other leaves aside.

• The giant water lily's leaves grow on long, strong stems. On the underside of each leaf is a web of supporting veins. This makes the leaves so strong that a toddler could sit on one without sinking!

Which are the smallest plants?

Although some types of algae grow to be the most enormous plants, there are other algae so small you can only see them through a microscope. The very smallest float in lakes and oceans, and are called phytoplankton. They're so tiny that whales catch millions in every gulp!

● The leaves and roots of water plants give food and shelter to many animals. But they're also places where hunters can hide.

Which forests grow in the sea?

Huge forests of kelp grow off the coast of California in the United States. Kelp is a kind of seaweed that grips on to rocks, and sends long ribbon-like stems up through the water. Some of the stems can be 200 metres long – as long as eight swimming pools laid end to end.

● Not all water plants are rooted in the mud. Some seaweeds float in the water, thanks to pockets of air in their leaves – rather like their very own rubber rings!

Which plant traps a treat?

When an insect lands on a Venus flytrap, it gets a nasty surprise! It only has to brush against one tiny hair on an open leaf tip, to make the leaf snap tightly shut. There's no escape for the poor insect. The flytrap changes it into a tasty soup, which it slowly soaks up.

● The bladderwort is an underwater meat-eater. Along its leaves are bubble-shaped bags, which suck in tiny creatures as they paddle past.

● Did you know that flytraps can count? The first time an insect touches a hair on one of the leaf tips, the trap stays open. But if it touches it a second time, the trap snaps shut!

one, two, three...

...fools a fly?

Pitcher plants have unusual vase-shaped leaves that tempt insects with a sugar-sweet smell. But the leaves are slippery traps. When a fly lands on them, it loses its footing, slips inside the 'vase', and drowns in a pool of juice.

● Many meat-eating plants grow on wet, boggy ground where the soil is very poor. They need their juicy snacks for extra nourishment.

...snares a snack?

The sundew's leaves are covered in hairs, which sparkle with glue-like drops. When an insect lands on a leaf, it gets stuck fast. The more it struggles, the more it sticks. At last, the leaf folds over, traps the fly, and starts dissolving it into liquid food that it can drink up.

Why do plants have flowers?

Many plants have colourful, perfumed flowers that attract insects and other animals. The visitors feed on drops of sweet nectar inside the flower. As they feed, they pick up a fine yellow dust called pollen, which they carry to another flower. When the pollen rubs off on the second flower, that flower can start to make seeds.

● This plant is called hotlips – and no wonder! The lipstick-red markings on its leaves are a wonderful way to attract visitors to its tiny flower.

● Many trees and grasses spread their pollen on the wind. They don't need animal visitors, so they don't grow bright flowers.

• Pollinators, such as this bat, don't mean to get pollen all over themselves. But a cactus flower is shaped in such a way that the bat just can't help it!

Which flower fools a bee?

A bee orchid's flowers look and smell just like female bees. Male bees zoom to the flowers wanting to mate with them – but they've been tricked! The plant's just using them as postmen to deliver little packets of pollen to other orchids nearby.

• During the summer, the air can be so full of pollen that it makes many people sneeze. Poor things – they haven't got a cold, they've got hayfever.

Which is the smelliest flower?

The dead horse arum is well named – it stinks of rotten meat! But blowflies love it. These plump flies usually lay their eggs inside the rotting bodies of dead animals. They're fooled by the plant's rotten smell, and crawl inside it to lay their eggs, picking up pollen on the way.

Why is fruit so sweet and juicy?

● The cotton-top tamarin lives in the South American rainforest. It feeds mainly on fruit, especially delicious, juicy figs.

Plants make sweet, juicy fruits so that animals will eat them. Inside every fruit is one or more seeds. When an animal swallows the fruit, it swallows the seeds as well. These pass through its body, and fall out in its droppings. In such good soil, the seeds soon start to grow into new plants!

● You often see seeds floating through the air. Dandelion seeds grow their own fluffy parachutes. And sycamore seeds have wings, which spin them to the ground like tiny helicopters.

Which plant shoots from the hip?

The Mediterranean squirting cucumber has a special way of spreading its seeds. As the fruit grows, it fills with a slimy juice. Day by day, the fruit grows fuller and fuller until it bursts, flinging the seeds far out into the air.

Which seeds sail away?

Coconut palms grow near the sea, so the ripe coconuts often fall into the water. Protected by their hard shell, they float out to sea. After several weeks or months, they are washed up on to a beach, where they sprout and start to grow.

● Fruits come in many different colours, but most animals seem to like red ones the best!

Which fruit gets forgotten?

Many animals feed on acorns, the fruits of the oak tree. Squirrels enjoy them so much that, every autumn, they bury some in the ground as a snack for when food is short in winter. The trouble is, the animals often forget where they've hidden their store, so when spring comes the young oaks start to grow.

When does a seed begin to grow?

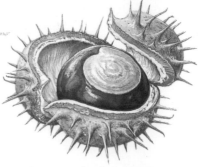

Inside every seed is the tiny beginning of a new plant. This starts to grow when the soil around the seed is warm and damp. At first, the baby plant feeds on a store of food inside the seed. But as soon as its first leaves open, it begins to make food for itself.

● The seed of the horse-chestnut tree has a tough brown coat. This rots away in the winter, and the young plant bursts through in the spring.

1 The bean seed swells with water, and splits open. A root starts to grow.

2 Tiny hairs grow out from the branches of the root.

3 A shoot appears. It grows up towards the light.

Do all plants grow from seeds?

Strawberry plants don't need seeds to produce new plants. They can send out side shoots, called runners. Where these touch the ground, roots begin to grow, then leaves and stems. In just a few weeks, there's a brand new plant!

● The coco-de-mer palm tree grows the largest seeds. They weigh 20 kilograms – as much as a big bag of potatoes.

Which plant grows the fastest?

The bamboo plant is the fastest-growing plant in the world. Some kinds can grow nearly a metre a day. At that rate, they'd reach the roof of a two-storey house in a single week!

4 The shoot grows leaves. Now the new runner bean plant can make food for itself.

● A cycad tree in Mexico must hold the record as the world's slowest-growing plant. After 120 years, it was only 10 centimetres high!

Are fungi plants?

Fungi aren't really plants at all. They look like plants, and they grow in the same sort of places. But, unlike plants, they don't have leaves, stems or roots, and they don't make their food from sunlight. A fungus grows by soaking up food from dead animals and plants.

● Scientists have found over 100,000 different kinds of fungi – and there are probably many more. These tiny bright blue toadstools grow in New Zealand.

What puffs out of a puffball?

A puffball is a kind of fungus that looks like a large creamy ball. If you knock a ripe one, a cloud of dust puffs out of the top. This dust is really millions of tiny specks called spores. Spores do the same job as seeds. If they land in rich soil, they will grow into brand new puffballs.

- Did you know that the blue bits in some cheeses are a kind of fungus?

- There were plants on land long before there were animals. Some of the kinds that plant-eating dinosaurs ate are still around today.

Which are the oldest plants?

Soft mosses and tall ferns first appeared on land about 350 million years ago. But the very first plants appeared on Earth more than 3,000 million years earlier. They were tiny, microscopic plants called algae, which floated in the sea.

- One kind of fungus not only feeds on dead animals, it kills them first! The tiny spores grow inside live ants, feeding on the juicy bits of their bodies. Soon, nothing is left but the ant's dry skeleton, with the toadstools growing out of it.

Why do trees have thorns?

Trees such as the acacia have thorns to keep plant-eating animals away, but they don't always work. Goats, camels and giraffes, for example, have tough lips and mouths and long, curling tongues to get round the thorns. The plants will have to come up with another trick!

● The leaves on the lowest branches of a holly tree are the prickliest, to stop animals nibbling them. Higher up, the leaves are out of reach, so they're a lot less spiny.

Why do stinging nettles sting?

Stinging is another way plants protect themselves. Each leaf on a nettle is covered with little hairs as sharp as glass. If an animal sniffs one, the hair pricks the animal's nose and injects a drop of painful poison – ouch! It won't stick around to eat that leaf!

Which plants look like pebbles?

● Milkweed is a poisonous plant, but the caterpillars of the monarch butterfly eat it and come to no harm. It even makes them poisonous – so they don't get eaten by birds.

Pebble plants grow in the desert in southern Africa. They have two fat, juicy leaves that any animal would love to eat. But the plant protects itself by blending in with the background. Its leaves are disguised to look so pebble-like that animals pass it by.

Which plants get a lift to the light?

In rainforests the tallest trees spread out their branches in the sunshine, making it shady down below. Because of this, some smaller plants don't get enough light. A group of plants called epiphytes have solved the problem by perching high on the branches of trees and growing up there instead.

Which plant has a private pool?

Bromeliads are epiphytes that grow high up on rainforest trees. They don't use roots to collect water – every time it rains, the plants catch drops of water in a pool in the middle of their leaves. The tiny pools are perfect for tree frogs to relax in, too!

- It's so wet in a rainforest that many plants have leaves with downward-pointing tips. They're like drainpipes for the rain to run down.

- Lianas are climbing plants that dangle from rainforest trees. Some animals use them as ropes, and swing on them through the trees.

- Not all epiphytes collect water in their leaves. Some, such as orchids, have long trailing roots, which soak up water from the steamy air like a sponge.

Which plants strangle and squeeze?

The strangler fig is well-named because it strangles other trees to death! Its seed sprouts high up on the branch of a tree. Week by week, its roots grow longer – wrapping round the branches, down the trunk, and into the ground. The fig now sucks all the goodness out of the soil, starving its host until it dies.

Can plants grow in a desert?

Plants can grow in a desert, but they need special ways to survive. Cacti have spreading roots that slurp up any rain as soon as it falls. Then they take great care of the water, storing it inside their fat juicy stems. It may have to last them weeks, months or even years.

● Desert plants save lives! Many thirsty travellers have sucked life-saving water from the juicy flesh of a cactus.

Can you pick fruit in the desert?

Huge bunches of sweet, sticky dates dangle from palm trees, beside springs in the deserts of Africa and the Middle East. People have been picking the delicious fruit in these parts for more than 5,000 years.

● A gila woodpecker makes a cool nest for itself by carving out a hole in a cactus. When it leaves, there's a long queue of other birds who'd like to move in!

Can you find flowers in the desert?

Daisies, poppies and many other plants flower in the desert. The plants wither and die during the hot, dry months, but their seeds survive in the ground. When it rains, they soon spring into action. They grow into new plants and cover the dry desert with a beautiful carpet of flowers within a few weeks.

Which are the tastiest plants?

Spices are made from plants. They have such a strong smell and taste that we use them in cooking to give food a kick! After being harvested, most spices are dried, and then crushed to a powder that you can add to your food.

● Spices are made from different parts of plants. Pepper comes from berries, cinnamon from bark, and ginger from a root.

● Most spices come from plants which grow in tropical parts of the world. For hundreds of years, merchants have travelled around the world to buy spices at markets like this.

Why do carrot plants grow carrots?

A carrot is a tasty food – but it's not really meant for us! Carrot plants live for just two years. In the first year they make food, which they store in a fat orange root. They use up the food in the second year, while they're growing flowers and seeds – as long as the carrots haven't already been picked!

● Roots, berries, leaves and seeds – plants give us so many wonderful foods that some people eat no animal foods at all. They are called vegans.

Do people ever eat grass?

Wheat, rice, corn, barley, oats and rye are just some of the grasses that people eat all over the world. We don't eat the leaves like cows and other animals do. We harvest the seeds. Then we either eat them whole, or grind them into flour to make pasta, bread and other important foods.

● Scientists can improve seeds so that they grow into stronger, healthier plants. This helps farmers to grow bigger and better crops.

What are old plants good for?

Three hundred million years ago, there were huge forests of trees and ferns. As the plants died, they fell into muddy swamps and were buried in the mud. Slowly, over millions of years, the plants were pressed down and turned into a black rock called coal. Coal is a fuel. We burn it in power stations to make electricity.

● The coal we burn today comes from plants that grew before there were even dinosaurs!

● Shampoos, perfumes, bath oils and creams are all made from sweet-smelling plants. That's how you smell so sweet!

● In some parts of the world, people run their cars on fuels made from corn, potato and sugarcane plants.

30

● The corks that seal bottles of wine are made from the bark of the cork oak tree.

● Many of the medicines we buy at the chemist's are made from plants.

CHEMIST

What are plants good for today?

Today's plants are still giving us the food and oxygen we need to survive. They also help us to make lots of useful things, such as paper, clothes and medicines. Every year, scientists discover new plants, and new ways to use them. So let's protect our plants.

● All sorts of useful things are made from rubber. It comes from the sticky juices of the rubber tree.

Cotton

Flax

● Cotton cloth is made from the soft hairs that surround the cotton plant's seeds. Linen is made from the stems of the flax plant.

Index